DEATH MASKS OF THE
RICH AND FAMOUS

DEATH MASKS OF THE RICH AND FAMOUS

WES CHESTLEYDALE

with

DUSTY TRICE

READ-◉-VISION

A PUBLISHING COMPANY · LOS ANGELES, CALIFORNIA, U.S.A.

ISBN Paperback: 979-8-9850737-6-8

ISBN Ebook: 979-8-9850737-7-5

Library of Congress Control Number: 2024934039

First paperback edition April 1, 2024.

Read-O-Vision, A Publishing Company
6450 Sunset Blvd. #1107, Hollywood, CA 90028
ReadOVision.com

For my adoring public.

In this world, nothing can be said to be certain except death and masks.

Wes Chestleydale

Contents

Introduction

Since the dawn of time, all living organisms have faced the exact same fate; the great irreversible termination of biological functions that, once unsustained, mean certain death. Over one hundred billion humans, or approximately 93.8% of all the humans to ever live, have died. Young, old, men, women, trans, nonbinary, rich, poor, health nuts, essential oil users, and flabby slobs. You, me, and absolutely everyone we know, will die. No one escapes death. No one.

When someone dies, we miss them. We grieve. We take clippings of their hair, cherish a picture or their favorite stuffed animal, or retain their pocket watches as treasured mementos to be passed down to future generations. Tangible remembrances of the departed are so very important to the living, because humans love knick-knacks.

But most dead people throughout history have been poor and their knick-knacks few. When these poor people died, often in dangerous farms, factories, or mines, they were quickly and unceremoniously dumped in holes to prevent the spread of disease and/or vampires. Then the memories of these poor souls would soon fade, and the remaining poor people would go back to work at the dangerous farms, factories or mines, until they too died, often tragically.

But some of the more fortunate dead people, members of the well-to-do glitterati of their day, died rich. These were the owners and/or beneficiaries of farms, factories, or mines. These rich people had nicer knick-knacks, often gold-plated. They could afford to be gently placed in much fancier holes, which I assume was also to prevent the spread of disease and/or vampires, but then again Dracula WAS a Count, and Counts ARE a type of very rich person, SO…

The rich could afford to shell out for lavish funerals. But they wished to be remembered for much longer and they wanted to leave behind much more valuable keepsakes.

By the 16th century, long before the invention of photography, rich people in Europe began commissioning paintings called mourning portraits (or deathbed portraits), depicting their recently deceased lying in repose on their deathbeds. These paintings were displayed for mourners at the funeral, and then sent home with the family to hang on the wall. Fine art, yes, but they weren't as popular as decorative paintings of flower arrangements or ships by the seaside, so very few examples have survived to this day.

During the 17th and 18th centuries, rich people paid to have highly realistic portraits made of the deceased to decorate their coffins. Aptly named coffin portraits, they were commonly painted on durable metal sheets shaped like the head end of the coffin. After a funeral, the coffin portrait would be removed from the rich person's casket and hung up on the walls of the church to show the very poor people that a very rich person had given the church vast sums of money.

But the thing about making paintings of the no longer living is that you can't dawdle. Corpses rapidly begin to smell and fall to bits, as decomposition happens rather quickly without refrigeration. It only stands to reason that the painters of deathbed portraits would have preferred to work with significantly fresher models. And nobody wants to look at a festering box full of that at a funeral. The process needed to be sped up and improved.

Enter the age of the death mask. A wax or plaster cast of a person's face taken soon after they died, but before they were rotting away and pushing up daisies, that could be used to represent the decedent at a funeral, then later kept as a memento. Painters and sculptors also used death masks as models for famous faces when painting posthumous portraits or sculpting souvenir statuary, without hurry or smell.

Casting a facial impression for a death mask is actually very similar to the process employed by modern Hollywood FX makeup artists when producing a latex facial appliance, only instead of the artist using a living movie star's head to make a mold, the impression for a death mask is taken from a no longer living corpse.

A dead person's face and hair would be greased down, often with olive oil, making it much easier for the mask maker to remove the completed mold from the deceased. Plaster bandages would be applied to the subject's head, with mask makers frequently dividing the mold down the middle, which sometimes left visible seams in the impression. Once dry, the mask would be removed and filled with metal, wax, or more plaster, leaving behind a near perfect cast of the deceased's face. If a death mask for a particular subject was in high demand, more copies could be made from the original, with finer features becoming muddier with each new casting.

Prepare yourself now to stare death in the face. What follows is a collection of death masks taken from history's greatest luminaries, both rich and famous, as lifelike as you've ever seen them before, or perhaps as you will ever see them again.

-Wes Chestleydale
January 29, 2024

Chapter 1
REST IN POLITICS

Including...
Aaron Burr
Benjamin Disraeli
James A. Garfield
William McKinley
Thomas Paine
Eva "Evita" Perón
Theodore Roosevelt

Aaron Burr (80)
February 6, 1756 - September 14, 1836

Claim to fame:
3rd vice president of the United States from 1801 to 1805, during Thomas Jefferson's 1st presidential term.

Location of demise:
Staten Island in Port Richmond, New York City, New York, U.S., in a boarding house later known as the St. James Hotel.

Cause of death:
Burr suffered two minor strokes in 1830 and 1833, and a debilitating third stroke in 1834 that left him partially paralyzed.

Final resting place:
Buried near his father in Princeton Cemetery in Princeton, New Jersey, U.S. No marker was erected until a plain marker was dedicated by a family member 20 years later. It was defaced.

Death mask maker:
Made by an unidentified artist for the New York phrenologists Fowler and Wells.

Last words:
Burr was an atheist and his last words were in response to his friend, Reverend P.J. Van Pelt, asking him to state that there was a God.
Burr replied. "On that subject I am coy."

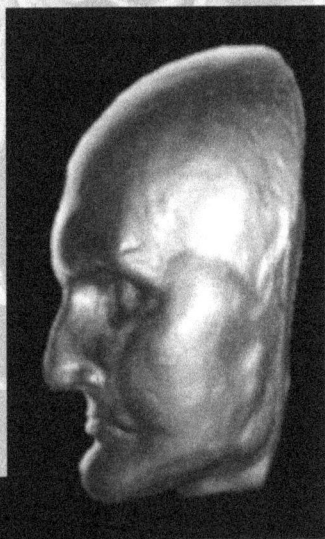

Aaron Burr
1756-1836

Benjamin Disraeli (76)
December 21, 1804 - April 19, 1881

Claim to fame:
Prime Minister of the United Kingdom.

Location of demise:
19 Curzon Street, Mayfair, London, England.

Cause of death:
Bronchitis. Because of asthma and gout, Disraeli went out very little, fearing more serious episodes of illness. He emerged from bed only for a meeting with other Conservative leaders on March 26th. The next morning, Easter Monday, he became incoherent, then comatose.

Final resting place:
Disraeli is buried with his wife in a vault beneath the Church of St. Michael and All Angels, which stands in the grounds of his home, Hughenden Manor in High Wycombe, Buckinghamshire, England. There is also a memorial to him in the church, erected in his honor by Queen Victoria.

Death mask maker:
Taken six hours after his death by Sir E. Boehm.

Last words:
"I had rather live, but I am not afraid to die."

Benjamin Disraeli
1804-1881

James A. Garfield (49)
November 19, 1831 - September 19, 1881

Claim to fame:
20th president of the United States in 1881.

Location of demise:
Elberon, New Jersey, U.S.

Cause of death:
After being shot by an assassin, once in the arm and once in the back, he died 80 days later of septic blood poisoning, a result of his doctors poking his wounds without proper sterilization.

Final resting place:
James A. Garfield Memorial, located in Lake View Cemetery in Cleveland, Ohio, U.S.

Death mask maker:
Augustus Saint-Gaudens.

Last words:
"This pain, this pain."

Fun facts:
The shooting occurred less than four months into Garfield's term as president. The assassin, Charles J. Guiteau, was convicted of Garfield's murder and executed by hanging one year after the shooting.

President James A. Garfield
1831-1881

William McKinley (58)
January 29,1843 - September 14, 1901

Claim to fame:
25th president of the United States, serving from 1897 to 1901.

Location of demise:
Buffalo, New York, U.S.

Cause of death:
Shot twice in the abdomen by an assassin. The president died of gangrene that grew on the wall of his stomach and poisoned his blood.

Final resting place:
McKinley National Memorial, Canton, Ohio, U.S.

Death mask maker:
Edward Pausch.

Last words:
First lady Ida McKinley sobbed, "I want to go, too. I want to go, too." Her husband replied, "We are all going, we are all going. It is God's way. His will be done – not ours."

Fun facts:
Leon Czolgosz, put on trial for murder nine days after McKinley's death, was found guilty and sentenced to death on September 26, and executed by electric chair on October 29, 1901.

President William McKinley
1843-1901

Thomas Paine (72)
February 9, 1737 - June 8, 1809

Claim to fame:
English-born American Founding Father, philosopher, political theorist, and revolutionary.

Location of demise:
59 Grove Street in Greenwich Village, New York City, New York, U.S.

Cause of death:
Unknown.

Final resting place:
Thomas Paine's corpse was taken to New Rochelle, New York, U.S., but the Quakers there would not allow him to be buried in their graveyard. Paine's remains were then buried under a walnut tree on the farm given to him by the state of New York as a reward for his Revolutionary era writings. In 1819, English journalist William Cobbett dug up Paine's bones and secreted them away to England, intending to rebury Paine in his native homeland. Cobbett's plan majorly backfired and the bones were still amongst his possessions when he died fifteen years later. Thomas Paine's skeleton was then lost, never to be recovered.

Death mask maker:
John Wesley Jarvis.

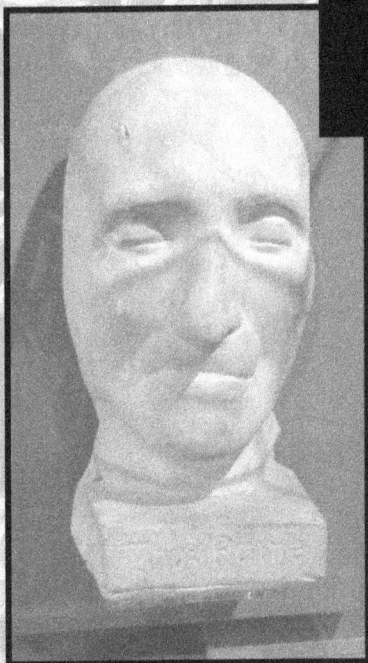

Thomas Paine
1737-1809

Eva "Evita" Perón (33)
May 7, 1919 - July 26, 1952

Claim to fame:
Argentine politician, actress, and philanthropist. First Lady of Argentina from 1946 to 1952 as wife of President Juan Perón.

Location of demise:
Unzue Palace, Buenos Aires, Argentina.

Cause of death:
Cervical cancer.

Final resting place:
La Recoleta Cemetery, Recoleta neighborhood of Buenos Aires, Argentina.

Death mask maker:
Juan Carlos Pallarols.

Fun facts:
Construction began on a monument larger than the Statue of Liberty to display Evita's body, but before its completion, Juan Perón was overthrown in a coup and fled the country. The new dictatorship removed Evita's body from display, and her corpse went missing for 16 years. Evita was found reburied in a crypt in Milan, Italy, under the name "María Maggi". Her face was smushed and her feet deformed from having been stored in an upright position.

Eva "Evita" Perón
1919-1952

Theodore Roosevelt (60)
October 27, 1858 - January 6, 1919

Claim to fame:
American politician, soldier, and naturalist, who served as the 26th president of the United States from 1901 to 1909.

Location of demise:
Died at his Sagamore Hill home in Oyster Bay, New York, U.S.

Cause of death:
Pulmonary embolism in his sleep. A blood clot detached from a vein and traveled to his lungs.

Final resting place:
Youngs Memorial Cemetery, Oyster Bay, New York, U.S.

Death mask maker:
James Earle Fraser, cast made at Sagamore Hill.

Last words:
Roosevelt's last words were "Please put out that light, James" to his family servant James E. Amos.

Fun facts:
Thomas R. Marshall, Woodrow Wilson's vice president, said that "Death had to take Roosevelt sleeping, for if he had been awake, there would have been a fight."

President Theodore Roosevelt
1858-1919

Chapter 2
MORIBUND MUSICIANS

Including...
- Ludwig van Beethoven
- Frédéric Chopin
- Franz Liszt
- Arnold Schönberg
- Franz Schubert
- Johann Strauss II
- Pyotr Tchaikovsky
- Richard Wagner
- Carl Maria von Weber

Ludwig van Beethoven (56)
Baptized December 17, 1770 - March 26, 1827

Claim to fame:
German composer and pianist, best known for
Piano Sonata No. 14, 'Moonlight' (1801) and
Symphony No. 5 in C minor, Op. 67 (1808).

Location of demise:
Vienna, Austria.

Cause of death:
An autopsy revealed Beethoven had significant
liver damage, which may have been due to his
heavy alcohol consumption.

Final resting place:
Beethoven was buried in the Währing cemetery,
northwest of Vienna. His remains were exhumed
for study in 1863, and moved in 1888 to Vienna,
Austria's Zentralfriedhof where he was reinterred
in a grave adjacent to that of Franz Schubert.

Death mask maker:
The painter Josef Danhauser made the death
mask only a few hours after Beethoven passed
away. Danhauser had to wait until a barber had
shaved Beethoven's face.

Last words:
On his deathbed, Beethoven was told of a gift of
twelve bottles of wine sent from his publisher.
His last words were, "Pity, pity—too late!"

Ludwig van Beethoven

1770-1827

Frédéric Chopin (39)

March 1, 1810 - October 17, 1849

Claim to fame:
Polish composer and pianist, best known for Nocturne in E flat, Op. 9, No.2 (1832) and Mazurkas, Op.24 (1836).

Location of demise:
Paris, France.

Cause of death:
His death certificate gave the cause as tuberculosis. Other possibilities include cystic fibrosis, cirrhosis, alpha 1-antitrypsin deficiency, or a rare case of pericarditis caused by complications of chronic tuberculosis.

Final resting place:
Père Lachaise cemetery, Paris, France.

Death mask maker:
Sculptor and painter Auguste Clésinger made Chopin's death mask and a cast of his left hand.

Last words:
"The earth is suffocating... Swear to make them cut me open, so that I won't be buried alive."

Fun facts:
As were his wishes, Chopin's heart was removed by his doctor, Jean Cruveilhier, and preserved in alcohol in a vase. It was given to Chopin's elder sister Ludwika who took it to Poland in 1850. Chopin's heart currently resides in Holy Cross Church in Warsaw, Poland.

Frédéric Chopin
1810-1849

Frédéric Chopin

1810-1849

Frédéric Chopin
1810-1849

Franz Liszt (74)
October 22, 1811 - July 31, 1886

Claim to fame:
Hungarian composer, pianist, conductor, and music teacher, best known for Dance Of The Dead (1838), Hungarian Rhapsody No. 2 in C# Minor (1847), and The Faust Symphony (1854).

Location of demise:
Bayreuth, Kingdom of Bavaria, German Empire.

Cause of death:
Terminal heart failure while suffering from pneumonia. In the last week of his life he began showing symptoms of terminal heart failure, including weakness, fatigue, anorexia, cough, difficulty breathing and delirium.

Final resting place:
Buried in the municipal cemetery of Bayreuth, Germany, against his wishes. It was a Lutheran cemetery, and Liszt was a devout Catholic.

Death mask maker:
Johann Christian Weissbrodt.

Last words:
"Please continue sleeping."

Fun facts:
Liszt played for the last time at a concert in Luxembourg on July 19, 1886.

happauf und Kästner 1886

Franz Liszt
1811-1886

Arnold Schönberg (76)
September 13, 1874 - July 13, 1951

Claim to fame:
Austrian-American composer, music theorist, teacher, writer, painter, and developer of the twelve-tone technique in the chromatic scale.

Location of demise:
Died at his home in Brentwood Park, Los Angeles, California, U.S.

Cause of death:
Diabetes, pneumonia, kidney disease, hernia, or edema. Take your pick. But also possibly Triskaidekaphobia, or the fear of the number 13!

Final resting place:
Wiener Zentralfriedhof (Vienna Central Cemetery), Simmering, Vienna, Austria.

Death mask maker:
Sculptor Anna Mahler, the daughter of composer Gustav Mahler.

Fun facts:
On his last day alive, Schönberg spent the day in bed, feeling anxious and believing the worst would soon happen to him. His wife, Gertrud, recalled: "About a quarter to twelve I looked at the clock and said to myself: another quarter of an hour and then the worst is over." Schönberg died on Friday the 13th at the age of 76. 7+6 = 13.

Arnold Schönberg
1874-1951

Franz Schubert (31)

January 31, 1797 - November 19, 1828

Claim to fame:
Austrian composer of the late Classical and early Romantic eras, known for Ave Maria (1825).

Location of demise:
In the apartment of his brother Ferdinand in Vienna, Austria.

Cause of death:
Typhoid fever (or possibly syphilis).

Final resting place:
At his own request, Schubert was buried near the grave of Ludwig van Beethoven, in the village cemetery of Währing, Austria. In 1888, both Schubert's and Beethoven's graves were relocated to the Zentralfriedhof in Vienna, Austria, where they are now located next to the later graves of Johann Strauss II and Johannes Brahms. Schubert's original grave in Währing Cemetery is now called "Schubert Park".

Last words:
"Here, here is my end."

Fun facts:
A year earlier Schubert had served as a torchbearer at Beethoven's funeral.

Franz Schubert
1797-1828

Johann Strauss II (73)
October 25, 1825 - June 3, 1899

Claim to fame:
Austrian composer known as "The Waltz King" for composing over 500 waltzes, polkas, and quadrilles, including The Blue Danube (1866) and Die Fledermaus (1874).

Location of demise:
Vienna, Austria-Hungary.

Cause of death:
Pleuropneumonia.

Final resting place:
Wiener Zentralfriedhof (Vienna Central Cemetery), Simmering, Vienna, Austria.

Last words:
Upon being told to get some sleep, Strauss uttered his final words: "I will, whatever happens." And then Strauss passed away.

Fun facts:
Johann's brother, Eduard Strauss, burned many of the Strauss family musical arrangements in 1909 to prevent the works from being claimed by another composer, chiefly Karl Michael Ziehrer. The music manuscripts were thought lost until conductors Alfred Walker and Klaus Heymann reassembled a semi-complete collection of Johann's works some 80 years later.

Johann Strauss II
1825-1899

Pyotr Tchaikovsky (53)
May 7, 1840 - November 6, 1893

Claim to fame:
Russian composer of the Romantic period, best known for Swan Lake (1877) and The Nutcracker (1892).

Location of demise:
Saint Petersburg, Russian Empire.

Cause of death:
Kidney failure, but also perhaps inconclusive. Tchaikovsky's death is attributed to cholera, caused by drinking unboiled water at a local restaurant. There is academic speculation that Tchaikovsky committed suicide, either with poison or by contracting cholera intentionally.

Final resting place:
Tikhvin Cemetery at the Alexander Nevsky Monastery, Saint Petersburg, Russia.

Fun facts:
Tchaikovsky was invited to visit the United States in the spring of 1891 for the inauguration of Carnegie Hall in New York City, New York, U.S.

On October 28, 1893, Tchaikovsky conducted the premiere of his Sixth Symphony, the Pathétique, in Saint Petersburg. Nine days later, he was dead.

Pyotr Tchaikovsky
1840-1893

Richard Wagner (69)
May 22, 1813 - February 13, 1883

Claim to fame:
German conductor and composer of operas, best known for Ride of the Valkyries from The Valkyries (1854) and the Bridal Chorus from the Lohengrin (1850).

Location of demise:
Ca' Vendramin Calergi, Cannaregio, Venice, Italy.

Cause of death:
Heart attack.

Final resting place:
Buried in the grounds of his home at Wahnfried, Bayreuth, Germany, in the tomb he had prepared for himself.

Death mask maker:
Augusto Benvenuti.

Last words:
The last words that Wagner ever wrote on a score: "Love -- Tragedy."

Fun facts:
After a funerary gondola carried Wagner's remains over the Grand Canal of Venice, Italy, his body was taken to Germany where it was buried in the garden of the Villa Wahnfried in Bayreuth.

Richard Wagner
1813-1883

Carl Maria von Weber (39)

November 18, 1786 - June 5, 1826

Claim to fame:
German composer, music critic, pianist, and guitarist, best known for his operas, including Der Freischütz (1821) and Oberon (1826).

Location of demise:
At the home of his friend and host Sir George Smart in London, England.

Cause of death:
Died in his sleep from tuberculosis.

Final resting place:
Originally buried in London, England. Eighteen years later, in December 1844, his remains were transferred and reinterred in the family burial plot in the Old Catholic Cemetery in Dresden, Germany, beside his youngest son Alexander, who died of measles at the age of 19.

Fun facts:
Carl Maria von Weber's widow originally gave his unfinished comic opera "Die drei Pintos" (The Three Pintos) to Giacomo Meyerbeer for completion. It was eventually finished by Gustav Mahler, who conducted the first performance in Leipzig, Germany on January 20, 1888.

Constanze Mozart, the wife of Wolfgang Amadeus Mozart, was a cousin of Carl Maria von Weber.

Carl Maria von Weber
1786-1826

Chapter 3
UNALIVE AUTHORS

Including...
Dante Alighieri
Fyodor Dostoevsky
Gustave Flaubert
Nikolai Gogol
James Hogg
Victor Hugo
James Joyce
William Shakespeare
Jonathan Swift
Leo Tolstoy

Dante Alighieri (56)
May, 1265 - September 14, 1321

Claim to fame:
Italian poet, writer, and philosopher,
best known for The Divine Comedy (1321).

Location of demise:
Ravenna, Italy.

Cause of death:
Quartan malaria contracted on a return trip from
a diplomatic mission to the Republic of Venice.

Final resting place:
Buried in Ravenna, Italy at the Church of San Pier
Maggiore (later called Basilica di San Francesco).

Death mask maker:
A copy of Dante's death mask has been on
display in the Palazzo Vecchio since 1911. It is the
current opinion of academics that it is not a true
death mask and was probably carved in 1483,
perhaps by Pietro and Tullio Lombardo.

Fun facts:
Florence, Italy regretted exiling Dante and
repeatedly requested the return of his body. At one
point the crypt keepers in Ravenna hid Dante's
bones behind a fake wall in their monastery.
Florence built a tomb for Dante in the Basilica of
Santa Croce in 1829. That tomb has never been
occupied, and Dante's remains remain in Ravenna.

Dante Alighieri
1265-1321

Fyodor Dostoevsky (59)
November 11, 1821 - February 9, 1881

Claim to fame:
Russian novelist, short story writer, essayist, and journalist, best known for Notes From A Dead House (1861), Crime and Punishment (1866), and The Brothers Karamazov (1880).

Location of demise:
At his home in St. Petersburg, Russia.

Cause of death:
Dostoevsky suffered a pulmonary hemorrhage. His wife Anna said that the hemorrhage had occurred after her husband had been searching for a pen holder he had dropped.

Final resting place:
Tikhvin Cemetery, Alexander Nevsky Convent, Saint Petersburg, Russia, near his favourite poets, Nikolay Karamzin and Vasily Zhukovsky.

Death mask maker:
Leopold Bernhard Bernstamm.

Last words:
Dostoevsky's last words were a quotation of Matthew 3:14–15: "But John forbad him, saying, I have a need to be baptised of thee, and comest thou to me? And Jesus answering said unto him, Suffer it to be so now: for thus it becometh us to fulfil all righteousness", and he finished with, "Hear now—permit it. Do not restrain me!"

Fyodor Dostoevsky
1821-1881

Gustave Flaubert (58)

December 12, 1821 - May 8, 1880

Claim to fame:
French novelist, best known for his debut novel Madame Bovary (1857) and the Three Tales (1877).

Location of demise:
Croisset (Canteleu), Rouen, France.

Cause of death:
Flaubert lived with venereal diseases most of his life. His health declined and he died at Croisset of a cerebral hemorrhage.

Final resting place:
Buried in Rouen Monumental Cemetery of Rouen, France in the Flaubert family vault.

Fun facts:
In his writings, Flaubert was very open about his sexual activities with prostitutes. He mentioned that he suspected that a chancre on his penis, a painless genital ulcer most commonly formed during the primary stage of syphilis, was from a Maronite or a Turkish girl he had met during his travels. He also engaged in sexual intercourse with male prostitutes in Beirut and Egypt, describing in one of his letters a "pockmarked young rascal wearing a white turban."

Gustave Flaubert
1821-1880

Gustave Flaubert
1821-1880

Gustave Flaubert
1821-1880

Nikolai Gogol (42)

March 20, 1809 - February 21, 1852

Claim to fame:
Russian novelist, short story writer, and playwright of Ukrainian origin, best known for Evenings On A Farm Near Dikanka - Volumes 1 & 2 (1831 & 1832) and Dead Souls (1842).

Location of demise:
Moscow, Russia.

Cause of death:
Starvation following extreme pre-Lenten fasting.

Final resting place:
Novodevichy Cemetery, Moscow, Russia.

Death mask maker:
Russian sculptor and artist Nikolai Ramazanov, whose memoirs about Gogol's death say:
"February 21 in the evening the doorbell rang in my apartment, and a very alarmed Mr. Aksakov appeared and announced Gogol's death. When I approached Gogol's body, he did not seem dead to me. The smile on his mouth and his open right eye gave me the idea of a lethargic dream, so I didn't suddenly decide to take off my mask."

Last words:
When Gogol was young, his grandmother told him a story about a ladder that took people's souls to heaven. The writer's last words were:
"The ladder, quickly, bring me the ladder!"

Nikolai Gogol
1809-1852

James Hogg (64)
December 9, 1770 - November 21, 1835

Claim to fame:
Scottish poet, novelist, and essayist, a.k.a. "The Ettrick Shepard", best known for The Private Memoirs and Confessions of a Justified Sinner (1824) and Noctes Ambrosianae (1822 to 1835).

Location of demise:
Altrive Farmstead, Ettrick, Selkirkshire, Scotland.

Cause of death:
Unknown.

Final resting place:
Ettrick Churchyard, Ettrick, Selkirkshire, Scotland.

Fun facts:
Hogg's most famous work, The Confessions Of A Justified Sinner, is thought to have influenced Robert Louis Stevenson's Jekyll And Hyde.

James Hogg was buried close to his childhood home in the Scottish Borders. In 2021, his grave and other graves in the cemetery were preemptively toppled by the Scottish Borders Council out of safety concerns. The decision to knock them over came after a 2017 Fatal Accident Inquiry into the death of an eight-year-old who was unfortunately killed by a falling gravestone.

James Hogg
1770-1835

Victor Hugo (83)
February 26, 1802 - May 22, 1885

Claim to fame:
French novelist, poet, and politician, best know for The Hunchback of Notre Dame (1831), Les Misérables (1862), and The Man Who Laughs (1869).

Location of demise:
Paris, France.

Cause of death:
Pneumonia.

Final resting place:
Panthéon, Paris, France.

Death mask maker:
Aime Jules Dalou.

Last words:
"Here is the battle of day against night. I see black light."

Fun facts:
Although he had requested a simple pauper's funeral, French President Jules Grévy awarded Hugo a state funeral by decree. The event was described by Friedrich Nietzsche as a "veritable orgy of bad taste." More than two million mourners joined Hugo's funeral procession in Paris from the Arc de Triomphe to the Panthéon, where he was laid to rest.

Victor Hugo
1802-1885

Victor Hugo
1802-1885

Victor Hugo
1802-1885

James Joyce (58)
February 2, 1882 - January 13, 1941

Claim to fame:
Irish novelist, poet, and literary critic, best known for Dubliners (1914), A Portrait of the Artist as a Young Man (1916), Ulysses (1922), and Finnegans Wake (1939).

Location of demise:
Zürich, Switzerland.

Cause of death:
Unexpected complications after undergoing surgery for a perforated duodenal ulcer.

Final resting place:
Fluntern Cemetery in Zürich, Switzerland.

Death mask maker:
Carola Giedion-Welcker had several casts made of Joyce's face. Swiss sculptor, Paul Speck made two original masks.

Last words:
"Does nobody understand?"

Fun facts:
James Joyce was originally buried in a standard grave, but in 1966 his corpse was reinterred at a more prominent location within the cemetery, with a statue of Joyce by American artist Milton Hebald added nearby. Joyce's wife Nora outlived him by 10 years, and was buried at his side, as was their son Giorgio, who died in 1976.

James Joyce
1882-1941

William Shakespeare (52)
April 26, 1564 - April 23, 1616

Claim to fame:
English playwright, poet, and actor regarded by many as the greatest dramatist of all time.

Location of demise:
Stratford-upon-Avon, Warwickshire, England.

Cause of death:
Unknown.

Final resting place:
Church of the Holy Trinity, Stratford-upon-Avon, Warwickshire, England.

Death mask maker:
Unknown. Alas, the death mask is also possibly a fake. This potential likeness of Shakespeare, known today as the "Kesselstadt death mask", was purchased by a German visiting London in 1775, and later found in a junk shop by German artist Ludwig Becker in 1849. Becker claimed the mask closely ressembled an existing painting of Shakespeare. Creedence was lent to the claim when Sir Richard Owen, a prominent anatomist and coiner of the term "Dinosaur", declared the mask authentic and said the Shakespeare memorial in Stratford-upon-Avon had been based on the mask. The mask is now generally believed to be much ado about nothing, though questions of its authenticity still linger.

William Shakespeare
1564-1616

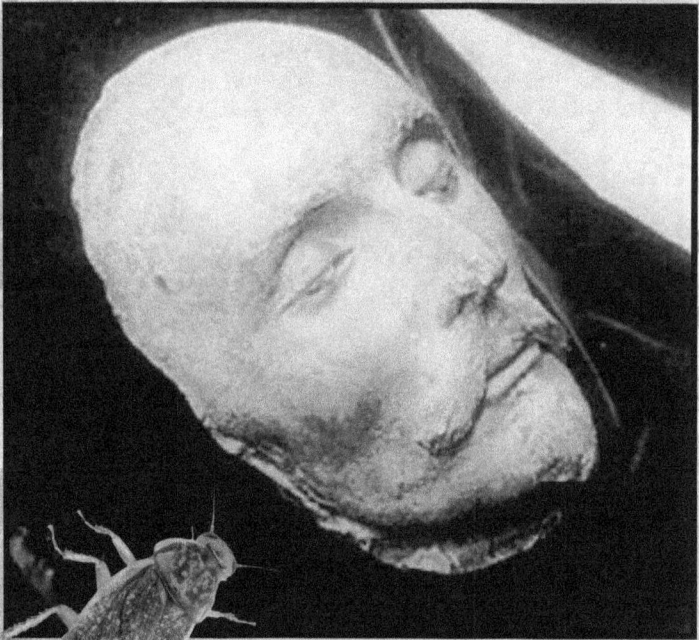

William Shakespeare
1564-1616

William Shakespeare's Famous Last Words

"The rest is silence."
    -Hamlet, *Hamlet*

"O true apothecary!
Thy drugs are quick. Thus with a kiss I die."
    -Romeo, *Romeo And Juliet*

"Yea, noise? then I'll be brief. O happy dagger!
This is thy sheath;
there rust, and let me die."
    -Juliet, *Romeo And Juliet*

"Et tu, Brute! Then fall, Caesar."
    -Julius Caesar, *Julius Caesar*

"A horse! a horse! my kingdom for a horse!"
    -King Richard III, *Richard III*

"Lay on, Macduff,
And damn'd be him that first cries,
'Hold, enough!'"
    -Macbeth, *Macbeth*

"I kissed thee ere I killed thee; no way but this,
Killing myself to die upon a kiss."
    -Othello, *Othello*

Jonathan Swift (77)
November 30, 1667 - October 19, 1745

Claim to fame:
Anglo-Irish satirist, essayist, poet, and Anglican cleric, best known for Gulliver's Travels (1726), and A Modest Proposal (1729).

Location of demise:
Dublin, Ireland.

Cause of death:
Stroke or terminal dementia.

Final resting place:
St Patrick's Cathedral, St Patrick's Close, Patrick Street, Dublin 8, Dublin, Ireland.

Death mask maker:
Unknown artist, commissioned by Dr. John Lyon.

Fun facts:
Swift wrote his own obituary in 1731, called Verses on the Death of Dr. Swift. He published it in 1739, fourteen years prior to his death.

Swift wished to be buried in his own cathedral, next to his "good friend" Esther "Stella" Johnson, who he was rumored to have secretly married.

He gifted the bulk of his fortune, £12,000, to create a hospital for the mentally ill, St Patrick's Hospital for Imbeciles, which opened in 1757.

Jonathan Swift
1667-1745

Leo Tolstoy (77)
September 9, 1828 - November 20, 1910

Claim to fame:
Russian writer and author of realist fiction, best known for the novels War and Peace (1869) and Anna Karenina (1878).

Location of demise:
Astapovo railway station, Ranenburgsky Uyezd, Ryazan Governorate, Russian Empire.

Cause of death:
Pneumonia and heart failure.

Final resting place:
Buried near the home where he was born, in Yasnaya Polyana (Bright Glade), Tula, Russia. Tolstoy called Yasnaya Polyana his "inaccessible literary stronghold."

Death mask maker:
Sergei Dmitrievich Merkurov.

Last words:
Tolstoy spent the final hours of his life on a train, preaching love, non-violence, and Georgism to the other passengers. When he arrived at Astapovo station, he was taken to the station master's home. His final words were spoken there. "But the peasants, how do peasants die?"

Leo Tolstoy
1828-1910

Chapter 4
LIFELESS LEADERS

Including...

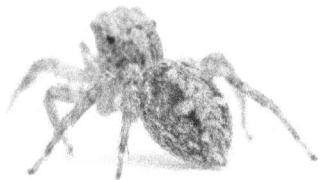

Napoleon Bonaparte (51)
August 15, 1769 - May 5, 1821

Claim to fame:
Emperor of France from 1804 to 1814, and 1815.

Location of demise:
Longwood House, St. Helena.

Cause of death:
Stomach cancer, but other possible causes include arsenic poisoning. Arsenic slows the decomposition of human tissue and causes "arsenic mummification." When Napoleon's body was moved in 1840, it was noted to be in extremely good condition. Preserved locks of Napoleon's hair have tested positive for arsenic.

Final resting place:
In 1861, Napoleon was reinterred in the crypt under the dome at Les Invalides in Paris, France.

Death mask maker:
Made by surgeon Francis Burton of Britain's Sixty-Sixth Regiment of Foot.

Last words:
"La France, l'armée, tête d'armée, Joséphine." ("France, the army, head of the army, Joséphine.")

Fun facts:
The doctor conducting his autopsy cut off Napoleon's penis. It is presently owned by a private collector in New Jersey, U.S.

Napoleon Bonaparte
1769-1821

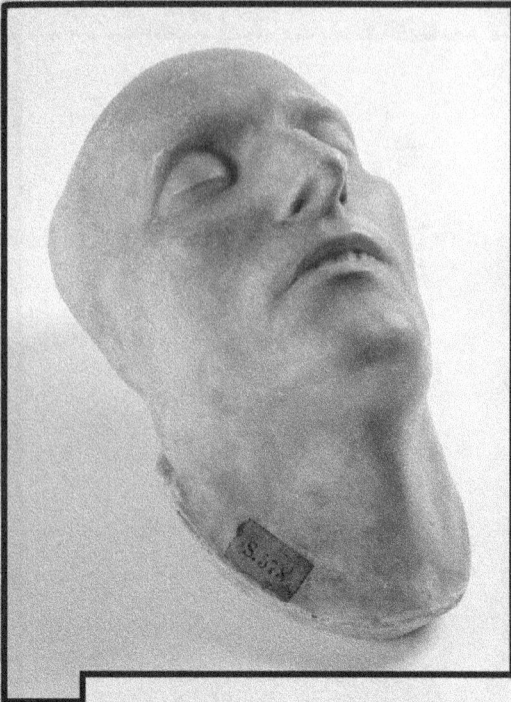
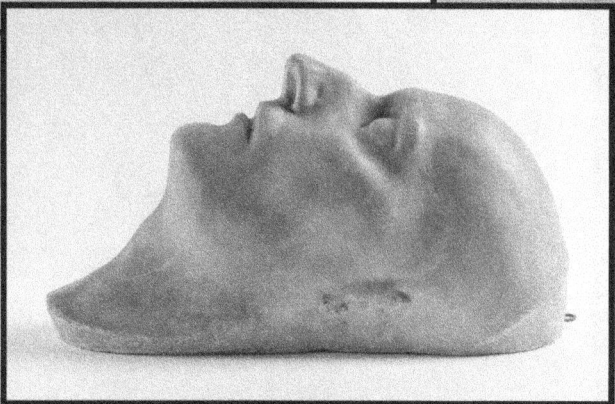

Napoleon Bonaparte
1769-1821

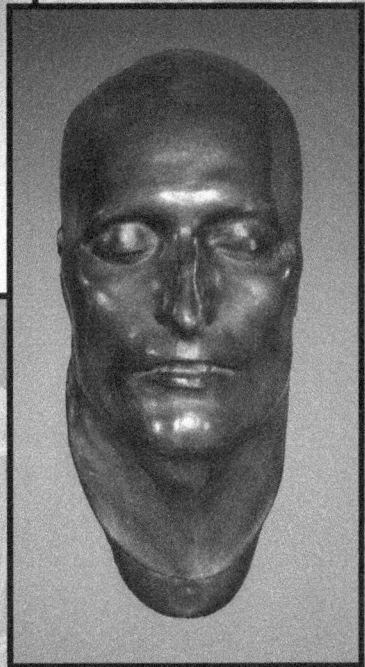

Napoleon Bonaparte
1769-1821

Oliver Cromwell (59)

April 25, 1599 - September 3, 1658

Claim to fame:
Lord Protector of the Commonwealth of
England, Scotland, and Ireland.

Location of demise:
Whitehall, City of Westminster, London, England.

Cause of death:
The most likely cause of death was sepsis (blood
poisoning) following a urinary or kidney infection.

Final resting place:
Buried at Westminster Abbey until Charles II
returned to the throne. Cromwell's corpse was
dug up on the 12th anniversary of Charles I's
execution. He was posthumously executed, his
body hanged in chains at Tyburn, London, and
then he was thrown into a pit. Cromwell's head
was placed on a spike outside the Tower of
London, where it stayed until 1685, then it was
reburied beneath the floor of the antechapel at
Sidney Sussex College, Cambridge, England.

Death mask maker:
Cast by Thomas Simon.

Last words:
"It is not my design to drink or to sleep, but my
design is to make what haste I can to be gone."

Fun facts:
Cromwell asked artist Samuel Cooper to paint an
accurate likeness of him, including his prominent
facial warts, coining the phrase "warts and all."

Oliver Cromwell
1599-1658

Franz Ferdinand (50)
December 18, 1863 - June 28, 1914

Claim to fame:
Austrian archduke whose assassination was the immediate cause of World War I.

Location of demise:
Sarajevo, Condominium of Bosnia and Herzegovina, Austria-Hungary.

Cause of death:
Assassinated by a gunshot to the neck at close range while being driven through Sarajevo.

Final resting place:
Artstetten Castle, Artstetten-Pöbring, Austria.

Last words:
"Sophie dear! Don't die! Stay alive for our children!" Count Franz von Harrach, who was in the car during the assassination, seized the Archduke by the collar, held him up, and asked, "Is Your Imperial Highness suffering very badly?" Ferdinand replied weakly, "It is nothing." ("Es ist nichts.") His voice grew weaker as he began to lose consciousness, he repeated the phrase six or seven more times, then died.

Fun facts:
The Austrian minister of finance received a warning of an assassination plot by the Prime Minister of Serbia, but the warning was ignored.

Sophie von Hohenberg (46)
March 1, 1868 - June 28, 1914

Claim to fame:
Wife of Archduke Franz Ferdinand of Austria, the heir to the Austro-Hungarian throne.

Location of demise:
Sarajevo, Condominium of Bosnia and Herzegovina, Austria-Hungary.

Cause of death:
Assassinated by a gunshot to the abdomen at close range while being driven through Sarajevo.

Final resting place:
Artstetten Castle, Artstetten-Pöbring, Austria.

Last words:
Sophie said to her husband, "For Heaven's sake, what has happened to you?!" Bleeding, she then fell forward, her face failing between her dying husband's knees.

Fun facts:
The bodies of Sophie von Hohenberg and Franz Ferdinand were transported to Trieste, Italy by the battleship SMS Viribus Unitis, and then on to Vienna by train. Their funeral was held at Hofburg Palace. They were then buried side by side in Artstetten Castle, the Habsburgs' summer home, because it was forbidden to bury Sophie in the House of Habsburg Imperial Crypt at Capuchin Church in Vienna, Austria.

Archduke Franz Ferdinand
1863-1914
Sophie, Duchess von Hohenberg
1868-1914

Franz Ferdinand and Sophie exit the
Sarajevo Guildhall on June 28, 1914.

The funeral service of
Archduke Franz Ferdinand and
Sophie, Duchess von Hohenberg.

Vladimir Lenin (53)
April 22, 1870 - January 21, 1924

Claim to fame:
Russian revolutionary, politician, and founder of the Russian Communist Party, who served as the first head of government of Soviet Russia from 1917 to 1924, and of the Soviet Union from 1922 to 1924.

Location of demise:
Gorki, Moscow Governorate, Russian SFSR, Soviet Union.

Cause of death:
Stroke. The official cause of death was an incurable disease of the blood vessels.

Final resting place:
Lenin's Tomb, Red Square, Moscow, Russia.

Death mask maker:
Sculptor Sergei Merkurov.

Last words:
Lenin, on his death bed, praised his dog for bringing a dead bird. "Good dog." ("Vot sobaka.")

Fun facts:
Lenin's mummified body was moved to Siberia for a four-year period during World War II.

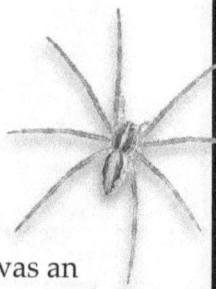

Vladimir Lenin
1870-1924

Lorenzo de Medici (43)
January 1, 1449 - April 8, 1492

Claim to fame:
Italian statesman, banker, ruler of the
Florentine Republic, and patron of
Renaissance culture in Italy.

Location of demise:
Died at the Medici family villa of Careggi,
Republic of Florence, Italy.

Cause of death:
Possibly acromegaly, a rare disorder that results
from excessive secretion of growth hormone.

Final resting place:
Lorenzo was buried with his brother Giuliano in
the Basilica di San Lorenzo, Florence, Città
Metropolitana di Firenze, Toscana, Italy. In 1559,
their bodies were interred in the New Sacristy in
an unmarked tomb beneath Michelangelo's
statue of the Madonna.

Last words:
"Pursue the line of conduct marked out by the
strictest integrity, as regards the interests of the
whole, nor the wishes of a part of the community."

Fun facts:
As Lorenzo de Medici died, a lightning bolt is
said to have struck the church of Santa Reparata.

Lorenzo de Medici
1449-1492

Peter The Great (52)
June 9, 1672 - February 8, 1725

Claim to fame:
Reigned jointly as co-Tsar with his half-brother Ivan V from 1682 until Ivan's death in 1696, Tsar of all Russia from 1696-1721, and the first Emperor of all Russia from 1721-1725.

Location of demise:
Saint Petersburg, Russia.

Cause of death:
In 1724 he had surgery to release four pounds of blocked urine. In early January 1725, he was diagnosed with uremia. During his autopsy his bladder was found to be infected with gangrene.

Final resting place:
Peter and Paul Cathedral in Peter and Paul Fortress, St. Petersburg, Russia.

Death mask maker:
Sculptor Carlo Bartolomeo Rastrelli.

Last words:
It is rumored that Peter asked for pen and paper on his deathbed and started to write a note that read: "Leave all to ..." Exhausted, he asked for his daughter Anna, then died a short time later.

Fun facts:
Empress Catherine I asked Rastrelli to make Peter's death mask, and molds of his hands and feet, which were used to make a wood and wax dummy that she dressed in Peter's own clothes.

Peter The Great
1672-1725

Joseph Stalin (74)
December 18, 1878 - March 5, 1953

Claim to fame:
Soviet revolutionary, politician, and leader of
the Soviet Union from 1924 to 1953.

Location of demise:
Kuntsevo Dacha, Moscow,
Russian SFSR, Soviet Union.

Cause of death:
Cerebral hemorrhage, and also his cerebral arteries
were severely damaged by atherosclerosis.

Final resting place:
Lenin's Mausoleum, Moscow, Russia (1953–1961),
then moved to the Kremlin Wall Necropolis,
Moscow, Russia (since 1961).

Death mask maker:
Matvei Genrikhovich Manizer, who was awarded
the People's Artist of the USSR in 1958.

Fun facts:
The stricken mass murderer was discovered by
his guards and maid, laying in his pajamas on his
dacha floor, having pissed himself. His
henchmen moved him to a sofa, but did not call
for a doctor. Some say Stalin used his last breath
to murmur angrily about wolves. Others say he
merely gurgled and gave people the stink eye.

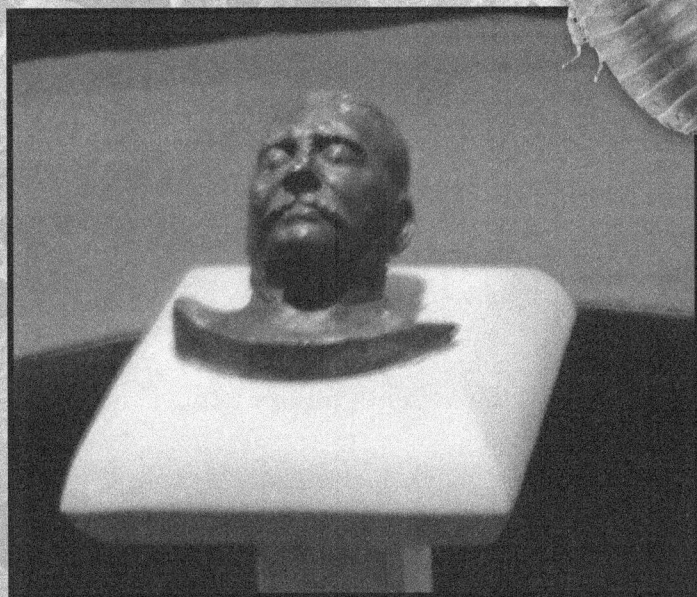

Joseph Stalin
1878-1953

Mary, Queen of Scots (44)
December 8, 1542 - February 8, 1587

Claim to fame:
Queen of Scotland from 1542 until her forced abdication in 1567, a.k.a. Mary Stuart.

Location of demise:
Fotheringhay Castle, Northamptonshire, England.

Cause of death:
Execution by beheading.

Final resting place:
Her body was embalmed and buried at Peterborough Cathedral. Her entrails were removed and secretly buried in Fotheringhay Castle. Her son, King James VI and I, ordered her corpse exhumed in 1612, and she was reinterred in Westminster Abbey, opposite the tomb of Queen Elizabeth I.

Last words:
"My faith is the ancient Catholic faith. It is for this faith that I give up my life. In Thee I trust, O Lord; into Thy hands I commend my spirit."

Fun facts:
The executioner held up her disembodied head by the hair and declared "God save the Queen." But it was quickly revealed that Mary's hair was only a wig when her head unceremoniously fell to the ground. Her real hair was short and grey.

Mary, Queen of Scots
1542-1587

Chapter 5
SCIENTIFIC STIFFS

Including...
Samuel Finley Breese Morse
Sir Isaac Newton
Alfred Nobel
Blaise Pascal
Louis Pasteur

Samuel F. B. Morse (80)
April 27, 1791 - April 2, 1872

Claim to fame:
Inventor of a single-wire telegraph system,
co-developer of Morse code, and
an American painter.

Location of demise:
New York City, New York, U.S.

Cause of death:
Pneumonia and old age.

Final resting place:
Green-Wood Cemetery in Brooklyn, New York.

Fun facts:
In 1871, a group of Western Union employees
devised a tribute to Morse, declaring June 10 as
"Samuel Morse Day." The celebrations included a
parade and the unveiling of a statue of Morse in
New York's Central Park. Morse appeared for the
grand finale and announced that he would be
saying goodbye to public life. A Western Union
operator tapped out Morse's farewell to the
nation via telegraph: "Greeting and thanks to the
Telegraph fraternity throughout the world. Glory
to God in the Highest, on Earth Peace, Goodwill
to men." Morse finished the telegraph message
himself by signing his name, S.F.B. Morse.

Samuel Finley Breese Morse
1791-1872

Sir Isaac Newton (84)
January 4, 1643 - March 31, 1727

Claim to fame:
English physicist, astronomer, and mathematician who was a key figure in the Scientific Revolution, and the formulator of the laws of motion and universal gravitation.

Location of demise:
Kensington, Middlesex, England.

Cause of death:
After suffering severe pain in his abdomen, possibly from bladder stones, Newton blacked out and never regained consciousness. He died in his sleep.

Final resting place:
Westminster Abbey, London, England.

Last words:
It is said that the dying Newton's final words were, "I don't know what I may seem to the world. But as to myself I seem to have been only like a boy playing on the seashore and diverting myself now and then in finding a smoother pebble or a prettier shell than the ordinary, whilst the great ocean of truth lay all undiscovered before me." But it is just as likely he actually said something more like, "Ouch! My bladder stones are back!" But that doesn't have quite the same gravity, now does it? Anyway, grain of salt.

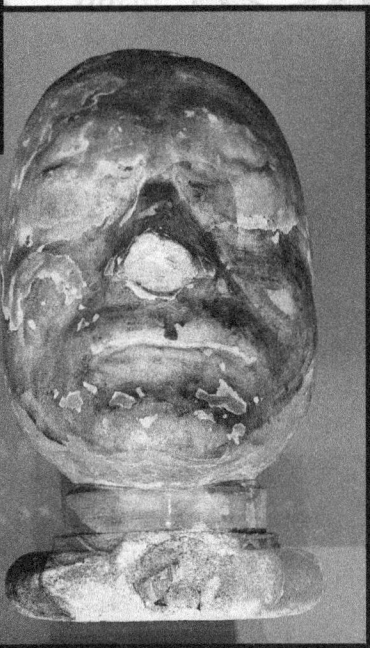

Sir Isaac Newton
1643-1727

Alfred Nobel (63)
October 21, 1833 - December 10, 1896

Claim to fame:
Swedish chemist, inventor, and engineer. Founder of the Nobel Prize, and inventor of dynamite.

Location of demise:
Sanremo, Liguria, Italy.

Cause of death:
Cerebral hemorrhage.

Final resting place:
Norra begravningsplatsen ("The Northern Burial Place" in Swedish), Stockholm, Sweden.

Fun facts:
Nobel was accused of high treason against France for selling a smokeless gunpowder called Ballistite to Italy, so he moved from Paris to Sanremo, Italy, in 1891.

Nobel outlined the creation of the Nobel prize in his last will and testament, which concludes, "Finally, it is my express wish that following my death, my arteries be severed, and when this has been done and competent doctors have confirmed clear signs of death, my remains be incinerated in a crematorium."

Alfred Nobel

1833-1896

Alfred Nobel
1833-1896

Alfred Nobel
1833-1896

Blaise Pascal (39)
June 19, 1623 - August 19, 1662

Claim to fame:
French mathematician, physicist, inventor, philosopher, and Catholic writer, known for inventing the syringe and the hydraulic press.

Location of demise:
Paris, France.

Cause of death:
Carcinomatous meningitis following a malignant ulcer of the stomach.

Final resting place:
The cemetery of Saint-Étienne-du-Mont, Paris, France.

Last words:
"May God never abandon me."

Fun facts:
As Pascal grew closer to the end, he asked to be sent to a hospital for incurable diseases. His doctors said he was too weak and unstable to be moved. Soon after, Pascal went into convulsions and died. An autopsy revealed several problems with Pascal's stomach and other organs, along with damage to his brain. The cause of his poor health was never definitively proven, but some have speculated it may have been tuberculosis, stomach cancer, or possibly both ailments.

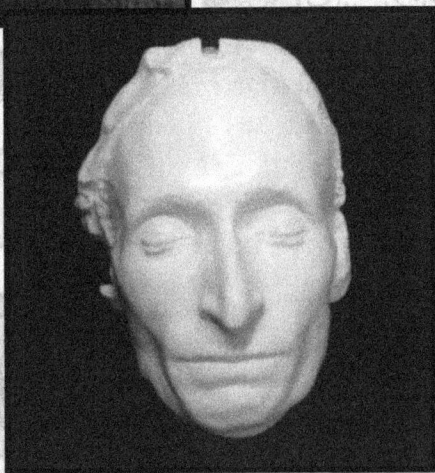

Blaise Pascal
1623-1662

Louis Pasteur (72)

December 27, 1822 - September 28, 1895

Claim to fame:
French chemist and microbiologist whose discoveries include the principles of vaccination, microbial fermentation, and pasteurization.

Location of demise:
Marnes-la-Coquette, France.

Cause of death:
Stroke or uremia.

Final resting place:
The French government had planned to bury Pasteur in the Pantheon, but Pasteur's wife/lab assistant Marie refused. Pasteur was then briefly buried in the cathedral of Notre-Dame in Paris, France, but his remains were relocated to a crypt at the Pasteur Institute in Paris, France in 1896. The ornate crypt had originally been a cellar used as storage for medical equipment.

Fun facts:
Louis Pasteur is credited with the development of the first vaccines for rabies and anthrax.

Pasteur, who laid the scientific foundations for the principles of hygiene, always avoided shaking hands. If at any point he made an exception to that rule and shook someone's hand, he would wash his own hands immediately.

Louis Pasteur
1822-1895

Chapter 6
CADAVEROUS CRIMINALS

Including...
William Burke
William Hare
John Dillinger
Charles "Pretty Boy" Floyd
Ned Kelly

William Burke (36?)
1792 - January 28, 1829

Claim to fame:
Committed sixteen murders over a ten month period in 1828 in Edinburgh, Scotland.

Location of demise:
Libberton's Wynd, Edinburgh, Scotland.

Cause of death:
Execution by hanging.

Final resting place:
Burke's skeleton hangs in the Anatomical Museum at Edinburgh University in Scotland.

William Hare (??)
Born between 1792 and 1804 - Unknown

Claim to fame:
Murderer who killed and sold corpses to an anatomist for scientific dissection in Scotland.

Location of demise:
Unknown.

Cause of death:
Unknown.

Fun facts:
Hare turned King's witness, was released from prison, and was never seen or heard from again.

William Burke (Death Mask)
1792-1829

William Hare (Life Mask)
Between 1792 and 1804-????

The Burke and Hare Murders
November 1827 to November 1828

The Gory Details:

William Burke and William Hare were murderers who killed at least sixteen people in Edinburgh, Scotland in 1828, and sold their corpses to an anatomist for dissection. On November 29, 1827, an old lodger died of dropsy in Hare's house, still owing Hare £4 in rent. Hare planned to steal the lodger's corpse from its coffin, with the help of Burke, and sell it to surgeon Robert Knox to recover the rent he was owed. Knox paid the men £7.5 for the body. In the coming months, Burke and Hare, along with their common-law wives, lured at least 15 more people into their lodging house, got them drunk, and smothered them to death. They then sold the corpses to Knox for study. The plot was exposed when two lodgers at the house became suspicious and found a local woman dead under a straw bed on Halloween night in 1828. Hare and his wife agreed to testify against Burke and his wife in exchange for being released. Burke was tried for murder, found guilty, and confessed. Burke exonerated Knox of the crimes. Burke's wife was released after the jury found the charges against her were not proven. Burke was hanged on the morning of January 28, 1829 in front of a crowd of 25,000+. The judge ordered Hare's body publicly dissected and anatomized, and his skeleton preserved.

William
Burke's
Skeleton

EXECUTION of the notorious WILLIAM BURKE the murderer, who supplied Dr KNOX with subjects.

Execution of Burke.
From a Contemporary Print.

William Burke's Execution

John Dillinger (31)
June 22, 1903 - July 22, 1934

Claim to fame:
American gangster during the Great Depression.

Location of demise:
In an alley near the Biograph Theater in Chicago, Illinois, U.S. Dillinger was pronounced dead at Alexian Brothers Hospital.

Cause of death:
Gunshot wounds. Dillinger was shot four times. The fatal bullet entered the back of his neck, severed his spinal cord, passed through his brain, and exited under his right eye, severing two sets of veins and arteries.

Final resting place:
Dillinger's body was put on display at the Cook County morgue, with 15,000+ people viewing the corpse over two days. Dillinger was buried in Crown Hill Cemetery, Indianapolis, Indiana, U.S.

Death mask maker:
Harold May of the Reliance Dental Manufacturing Co. created this death mask at the Cook County Morgue in Chicago, Illinois, U.S.

Fun facts:
The Biograph Theater was showing *Manhattan Melodrama*, featuring Clark Gable and Myrna Loy.

ORIGINAL DEATH MASK & HAIR

This plaster casting was one of the originals prepared from Dillinger's body at the Cook County Morgue. Purportedly, the FBI confiscated the first mold, but others were taken without their knowledge.

Look closely down at the magnifier lens, it contains a hair from Dillinger's eyebrow encrusted from the mold.

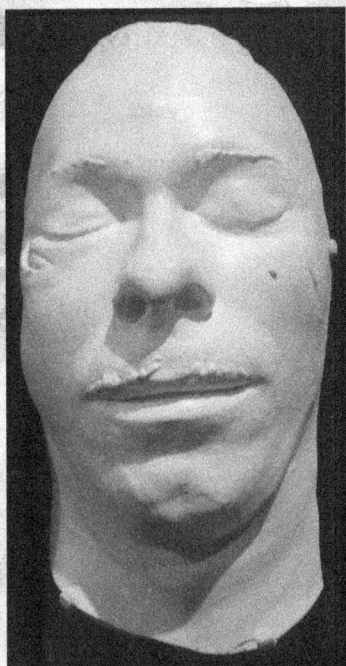

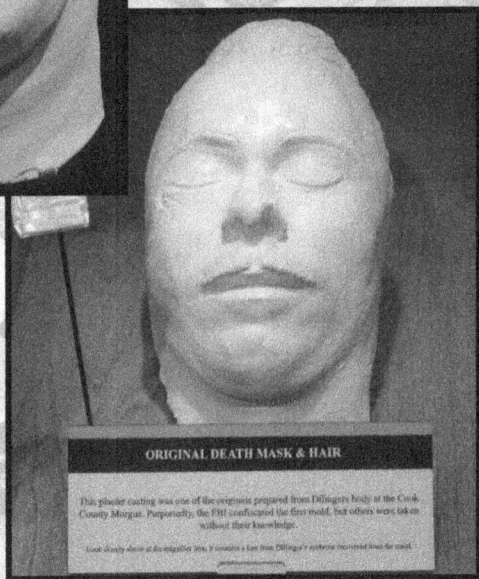

John Dillinger
1903-1934

Charles "Pretty Boy" Floyd (30)
February 3, 1904 - October 22, 1934

Claim to fame:
American bank robber.

Location of demise:
East Liverpool, Ohio, U.S.

Cause of death:
Multiple gunshot wounds.

Final resting place:
Floyd's body was taken to the nearest funeral home, the Sturgis Funeral Home in East Liverpool, Ohio, U.S. where it was embalmed and put on display. Floyd's corpse was again put on public display in Sallisaw, Oklahoma, U.S. According to the Oklahoma Historical Society, his funeral was attended by over 20,000 people and remains the largest funeral in Oklahoma history. He was buried in Akins, Oklahoma, U.S.

Death mask maker:
Frank Dawson embalmed Floyd and made his death mask out of slip, a clay slurry used to make pottery. His death mask remains at the Sturgis Funeral Home, now a bed & breakfast, where it is displayed in a basement laundry room.

Last words:
"I'm done for. You've hit me twice."

Charles "Pretty Boy" Floyd
1904-1934

Ned Kelly (25)
December 1854 - November 11, 1880

Claim to fame:
Australian bushranger, outlaw, gang leader, and convicted police-murderer.

Location of demise:
Old Melbourne Gaol, Melbourne, Colony of Victoria, Australia.

Cause of death:
Execution by hanging.

Final resting place:
Kelly was initially buried at the Old Melbourne Gaol graveyard. When the Old Melbourne Gaol closed, his body was exhumed. His bones were stolen by bystanders as souvenirs, but later returned, and he was reburied in a mass grave at Pentridge Prison in Coburg. His skull was not reburied and was stolen again in 1978. In 2013, Kelly's headless body was reburied in an unmarked grave within Greta Cemetery, Greta, Wangaratta Rural City, Victoria, Australia. The whereabouts of Kelly's skull remains a mystery.

Death mask maker:
Waxworks proprietor Maximilian Kreitmayer.

Last words:
"Ah, well, I suppose it has come to this."

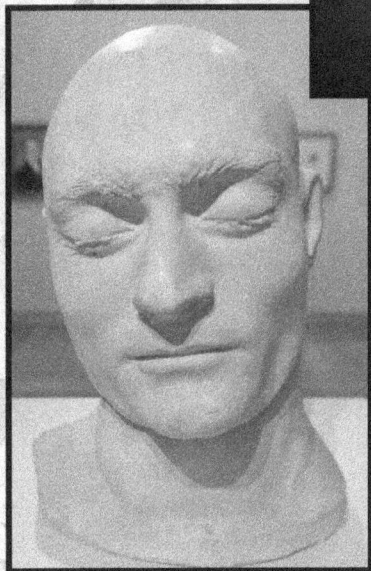

Ned Kelly
1854-1880

Chapter 7
FORMER MILITARY

Including...
George Dewey
Ulysses S. Grant
Heinrich Himmler
Robert E. Lee
Erwin Rommel
William Tecumseh Sherman
Francisco 'Pancho' Villa
Emiliano Zapata

George Dewey (79)
December 26, 1837 - January 16, 1917

Claim to fame:
Admiral of the Navy, the highest-possible
rank in the United States Navy.

Location of demise:
He lived at 1730 K Street NW, in Washington,
D.C., U.S. for the last 17 years of his life, and died
at his home.

Cause of death:
Old age, after a week of illness.

Final resting place:
After lying in state at the United States Capitol
rotunda, he was buried at Arlington National
Cemetery. A mausoleum was later built for him
within the cemetery. In 1925, his widow had his
remains transferred to the Bethlehem Chapel, on
the crypt level, at the Washington National
Cathedral, Washington, D.C., U.S.

Death mask maker:
Ulric Stonewall Jackson "U.S.J." Dunbar.

Fun facts:
Dewey explored a run for the 1900 Democratic
presidential nomination, but withdrew from the
race and endorsed President William McKinley.

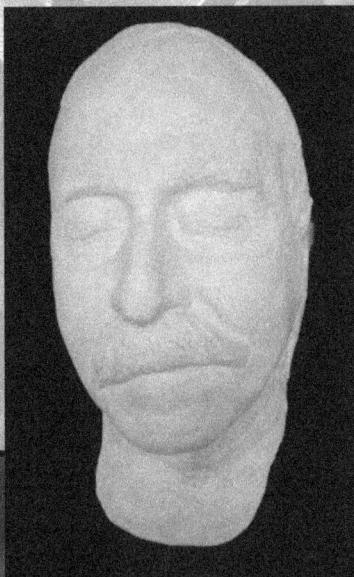

Admiral George Dewey
1837-1917

Ulric Stonewall Jackson
"U.S.J." Dunbar works on the death
mask of Admiral George Dewey.

Ulric Stonewall Jackson
"U.S.J." Dunbar displays the
completed death mask of
Admiral George Dewey.

Ulysses S. Grant (63)
April 27, 1822 - July 23, 1885

Claim to fame:
Commanding general of the U.S. Army from 1864 to 1869, and 18th president of the United States from 1869 to 1877.

Location of demise:
Mount McGregor cottage, Wilton, New York, U.S.

Cause of death:
Throat cancer, possibly caused by cigar smoking.

Final resting place:
Grant's Tomb, New York City, New York, U.S.

Death mask maker:
Plaster cast made by Karl Gerhardt.

Last words:
"Water." Shortly before his death, Grant was also said to have written, "There was never one more willing to go than I am."

Fun facts:
Death Mask maker Karl Gerhardt wrote to Samuel Clemens (Mark Twain) a few days after Grant's death to say that guards had to be posted at Grant's cottage to keep out overzealous sculptor Rupert Schmid, who said "he would have a mask at any cost", and had called Gerhardt unqualified to make such an important work.

President Ulysses S. Grant
1822-1885

Heinrich Himmler (44)
October 7, 1900 - May 23, 1945

Claim to fame:
Leading member of the Nazi Party of Germany,
known for being a main architect of the Holocaust.

Location of demise:
The headquarters of the Second British Army in
Lüneburg, Germany.

Cause of death:
Suicide by cyanide poisoning after biting a
potassium cyanide pill when he was captured.

Final resting place:
An unmarked grave near Lüneburg, Germany.

Death mask maker:
Made by either Sergeant John St George Glyn or a
dentist sent to take molar impressions of Himmler.

Last words:
According to the written account of Corporal
Harry Oughton Jones, a member of the Durham
Light Infantry Regiment, Himmler said, "You my
boy are just a young captain and to take me I
want to see your colonel in charge." Himmler
then laughed, took the potassium cyanide pill,
kicked two or three times, and lay still.

Fun facts:
Himmler had shaved off his mustache, and was
disguised in a sergeant's uniform and eye patch.

Heinrich Himmler
1900-1945

Robert E. Lee (63)

January 19, 1807 - October 12, 1870

Claim to fame:
Confederate general during the American Civil War.

Location of demise:
Lexington, Virginia, U.S.

Cause of death:
Lee had a stroke and died two weeks later from pneumonia.

Final resting place:
University Chapel at Washington and Lee University, Lexington, Virginia, U.S.

Death mask maker:
American sculptor Clark Mills.

Last words:
It was written that he said, "Tell Hill he must come up! Strike the tent," but this has been disputed as Lee could only utter monosyllables at the end of his life due to a stroke.

Fun facts:
When Lee died, the roads to Lexington had just flooded, and the caskets the undertaker ordered were all washed away down the Maury River. Two boys located one of the undamaged coffins downriver, but the coffin was too short for the 5 foot 10 inch Lee, so he was buried without shoes.

General Robert E. Lee
1807-1870

Erwin Rommel (52)

November 15, 1891 - October 14, 1944

Claim to fame:
German field marshal during World War II, popularly known as "The Desert Fox".

Location of demise:
Herrlingen, Gau Württemberg-Hohenzollern, Nazi Germany.

Cause of death:
Forced suicide by cyanide poisoning.

Final resting place:
Herrlingen cemetery, Herrlingen, Alb-Donau-Kreis, Baden-Württemberg, Germany.

Death mask maker:
A former fellow officer, who served with Rommel in WWI, commissioned the death mask.

Last words:
"To die at the hands of one's own people is hard, but the house is surrounded and Hitler is charging me with high treason." Rommel told his 15-year-old son Manfred minutes before he left their house for the last time.

Fun facts:
Rommel's name came up during an investigation into a foiled plot to assassinate Hitler. Hitler offered Rommel the chance to take his own life and be buried with honor rather than face a trial.

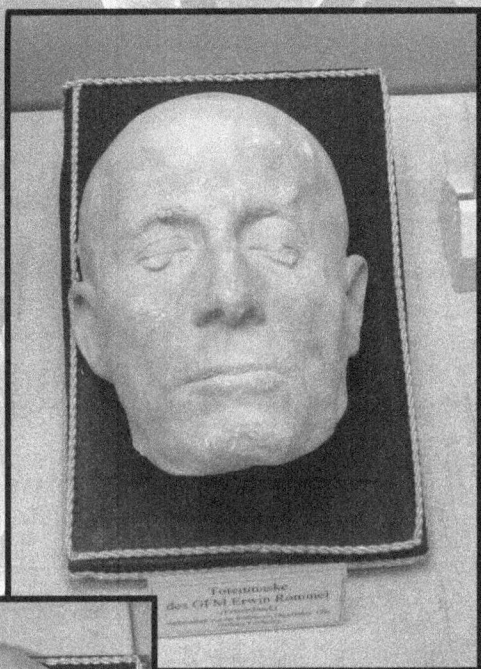

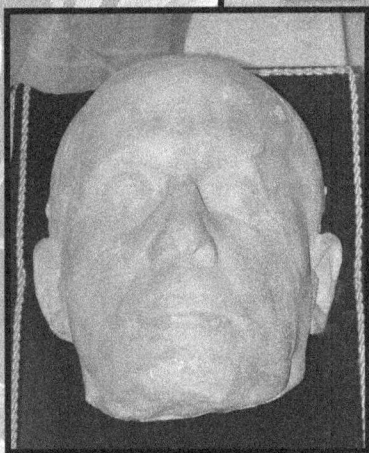

Erwin Rommel

1891-1944

William Tecumseh Sherman (71)
February 8, 1820 - February 14, 1891

Claim to fame:
American soldier, businessman, and author who served as a general in the Union Army during the American Civil War from 1861 to 1865.

Location of demise:
New York City, New York, U.S.

Cause of death:
Pneumonia.

Final resting place:
Calvary Cemetery, St. Louis, Missouri, U.S.

Death mask maker:
Mask made by Daniel Chester French, who went on to design the statue of Abraham Lincoln in the Lincoln Memorial three decades later.

Fun facts:
The Confederate general who commanded the resistance to Sherman's troops in Georgia and the Carolinas, Joseph E. Johnston, served as a pallbearer at Sherman's funeral. It was bitterly cold in New York and Johnston's friend, fearing that Johnston might catch a cold, told him to put on a hat. Johnston replied: "If I were in [Sherman's] place, and he were standing in mine, he would not put on his hat." Johnston caught a serious cold and died one month later of pneumonia.

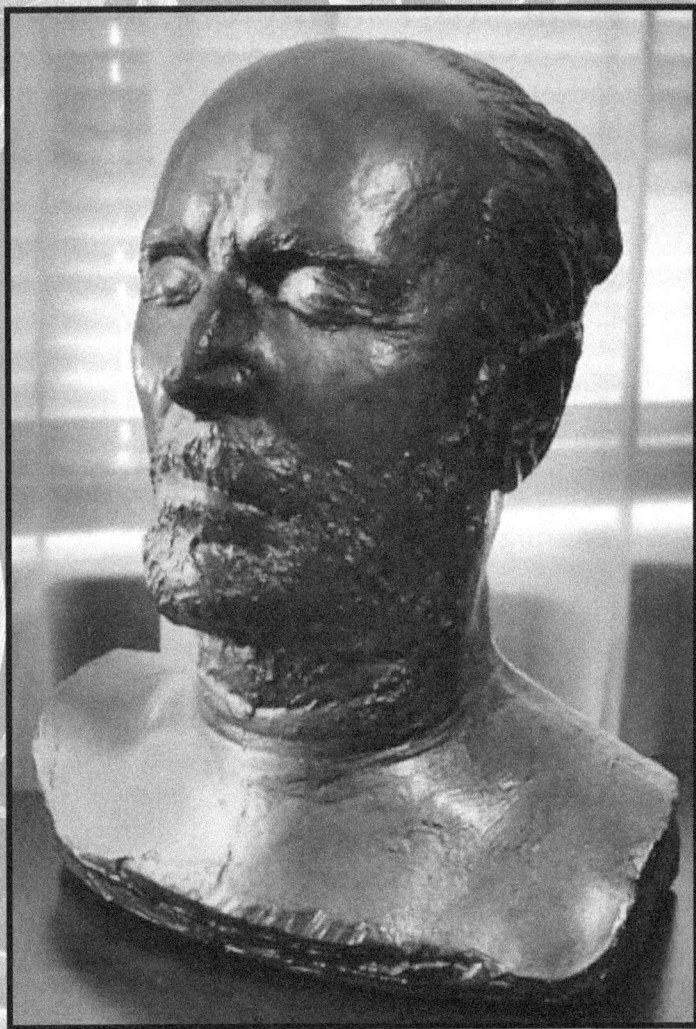

William Tecumseh Sherman
1820-1891

Francisco 'Pancho' Villa (45)
June 5, 1878 - July 20, 1923

Claim to fame:
General in the Mexican Revolution.

Location of demise:
Parral, Chihuahua, Mexico.

Cause of death:
Assassinated in a hail of bullets while traveling home by car from a visit to Parral, Mexico, most likely on the orders of political enemies Plutarco Elías Calles and President Alvaro Obregón.

Final resting place:
Monument to the Revolution, Cuauhtémoc borough, Mexico City, Mexico.

Last words:
According to the lone survivor of the attack, Ramon Contreras, Villa's last words were, "Don't let it end like this. Tell them I said something." But two days after the assassination, Contreras was interviewed and said that Villa had died within seconds of the attack and did not have time to say much of anything.

Fun facts:
Pancho Villa was born José Doroteo Arango Arámbula. The nickname Pancho Villa is believed to be similar to a bandit leader he had met or perhaps even Villa's grandfather's last name.

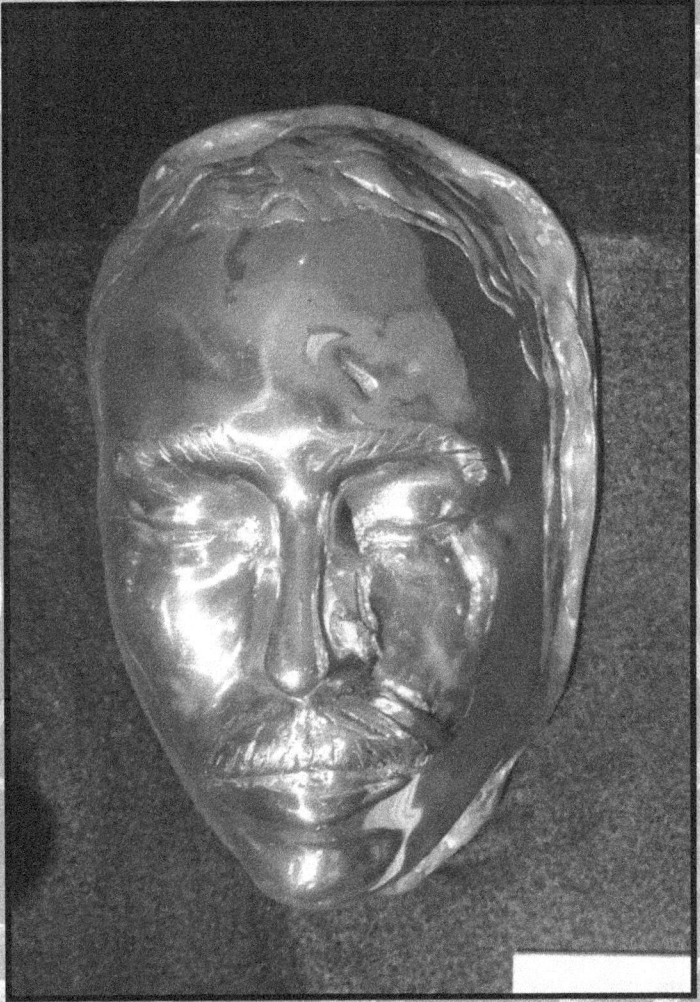

Francisco 'Pancho' Villa
1878-1923

Emiliano Zapata (39)
August 8, 1879 - April 10, 1919

Claim to fame:
A leading figure in the Mexican Revolution.

Location of demise:
Hacienda de San Juan, Chinameca, Ayala municipality, Morelos, Mexico.

Cause of death:
Gunshot wounds after he was tricked, ambushed, and killed by government forces.

Final resting place:
Monumento a Emiliano Zapata
Cuautla Morelos, Cuautla, Morelos, Mexico.

Fun facts:
In 1916, Mexican President Carranza sent General Pablo Garza to Morelos to destroy the Zapatistas. Zapata's supporters were to be killed or deported as slave laborers. Zapata survived and fought back against the Carrancistas. But in early 1919, a Mexican colonel named Jesus Guajardo suggested he was ready to defect with men and weapons. Zapata tested Guajardo, and decided to meet with him. When Zapata arrived at the meeting, he was ambushed and killed by Guajardo's men.

Emiliano Zapata originated the saying, "Prefiero morir de pie que vivir de rodillas," which translates as "I prefer to die on my feet than live on my knees."

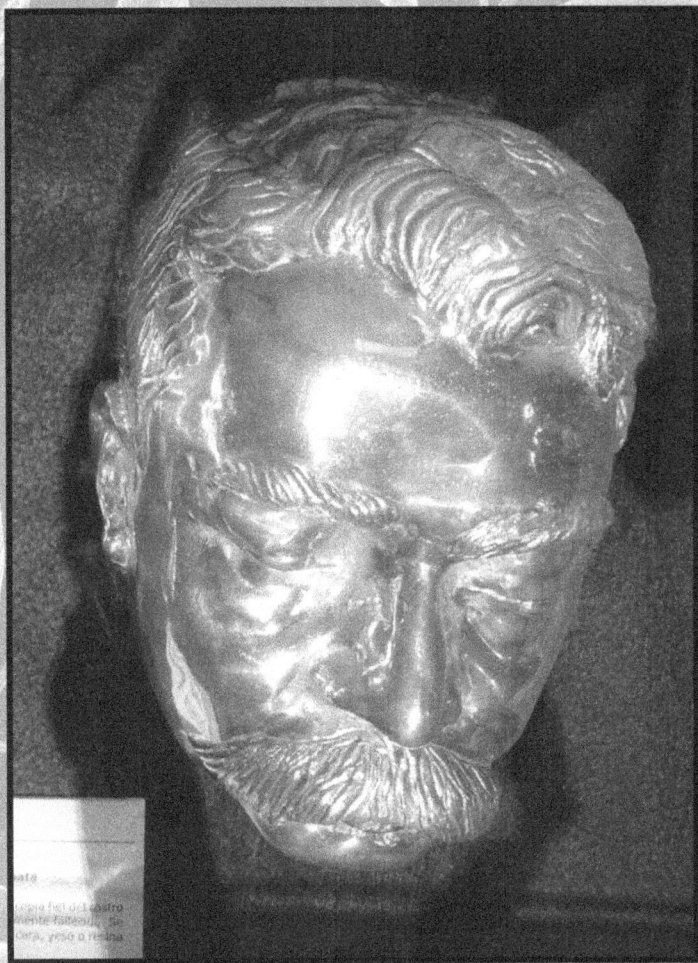

Emiliano Zapata
1879-1919

Chapter 8
STONE COLD CLERGY

Including...
  Martin Luther
  Pope Pius IX
  Hyrum Smith
  Joseph Smith
  John Wesley

Martin Luther (62)

November 10, 1483 - February 18, 1546

Claim to fame:
German priest, theologian, and key figure of the Protestant Reformation whose beliefs form the basis of Lutheranism.

Location of demise:
Eisleben, County of Mansfeld, Saxony, Holy Roman Empire, now in Anhalt, Germany.

Cause of death:
Heart attack.

Final resting place:
Schlosskirche (Castle Church) in Wittenberg, Germany, in front of a wooden pulpit in the center of the church, about six feet down.

Death mask maker:
Painter Lukas Furtenagel. Modifications were made to the original mask, such as opening the eyelids. In 1926, the anthropologist Hans Hahne reconstructed Luther's original death mask.

Last words:
"For God so loved the world that he gave his only son." Luther's friend Dr. Jonas knew what was happening and asked Luther, "Do you want to die standing firm on Christ and the doctrine you have taught?" Luther replied, "Yes."

Fun facts:
Holy Roman Emperor Charles V ordered his troops not to disturb Martin Luther's grave.

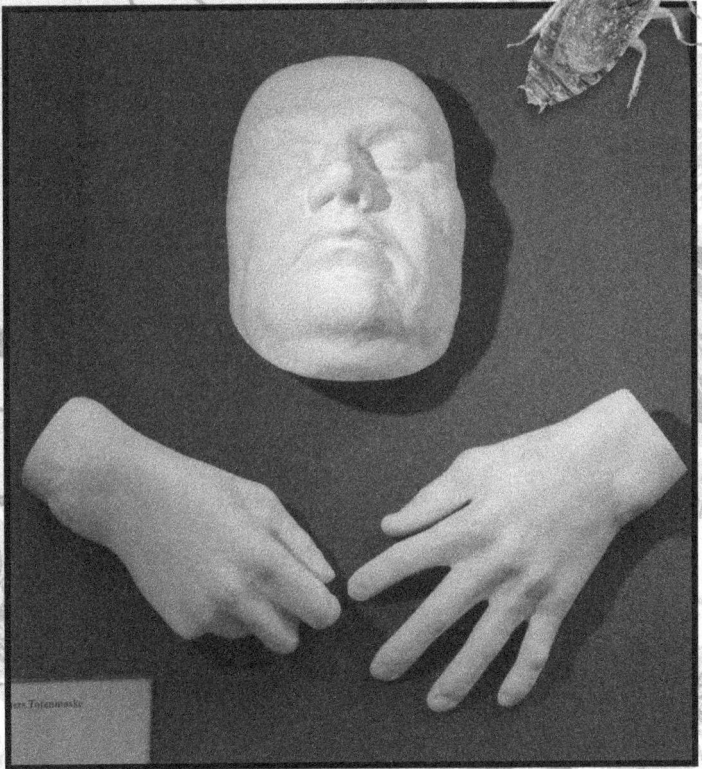

Martin Luther
1483-1546

Pope Pius IX (85)
May 13, 1792 - February 7, 1878

Claim to fame:
Head of the Catholic Church from 1846 to 1878, the longest verified papal reign.

Location of demise:
Apostolic Palace, Vatican City, Kingdom of Italy.

Cause of death:
Epileptic seizure and a sudden heart attack.

Final resting place:
Originally buried in Saint Peter's grotto, but later moved to the Basilica of Saint Lawrence outside the Vatican City walls in Rome, Italy.

Last words:
"Guard the Church I loved so well and sacredly."

Fun facts:
In the middle of the night of July 13, 1881, Pope Pius IX was moved from Saint Peter's grotto. When the procession came to the Tiber River, a group of anticlerical Romans abushed them, screaming, "Long live Italy! Death to the Pope! Death to the Priests!" The mob threatened to throw the coffin into the river, but a militia arrived in the knick of time and stopped them. After his beatification, Pius IX's simple grave was upgraded at the behest of Pope John Paul II.

Pope Pius IX
1792-1878

Hyrum Smith (44)
February 9, 1800 - June 27, 1844

Claim to fame:
American religious leader in the Church of
Jesus Christ of Latter Day Saints.

Location of demise:
Carthage, Illinois, U.S.

Cause of death:
An armed mob of 60-200 men with blackened
faces stormed Carthage Jail, where Hyrum and
his brother Joseph were being detained in the
jailer's bedroom. Hyrum was in the process of
attempting to barricade the door and was killed
instantly when he was shot in the face just to
the left side of his nose. He staggered backward
and another ball fired through the window
struck him in the back, passed through his
body, and struck the watch in his vest pocket.

Final resting place:
Smith Family Cemetery, Nauvoo, Illinois, U.S.

Death mask maker:
The death masks of both Hyrum and Joseph Smith
were made by George Cannon, a furniture maker
who also served as the local undertaker since he
made coffins as well as cabinets. Plasterer William
Rowley, made the positive images from the molds.

Last words:
"I am a dead man."

Joseph Smith (38)

December 23, 1805 - June 27, 1844

Claim to fame:
American religious leader, and the founder of Mormonism and the Latter Day Saint movement.

Location of demise:
Carthage, Illinois, U.S.

Cause of death:
Joseph was shot multiple times by a mob before falling out an open window. He died shortly after hitting the ground, but was shot several more times by a firing squad before the mob dispersed.

Final resting place:
Smith Family Cemetery, Nauvoo, Illinois, U.S.

Last words:
"Oh Lord my God!"

Fun facts:
As mayor of Nauvoo, Illinois, U.S., Smith ordered the destruction of a non-Mormon newspaper critical of church leaders. The Smith brothers were charged with inciting a riot, but warrants were dismissed by Nauvoo courts. Smith declared martial law in Nauvoo and fled Illinois. The Smiths voluntarily surrendered to authorities in Carthage, where they were also charged with treason against Illinois for declaring martial law. They were killed by a mob while awaiting trial.

Joseph Smith published the Book of Mormon when he was only 24 years of age.

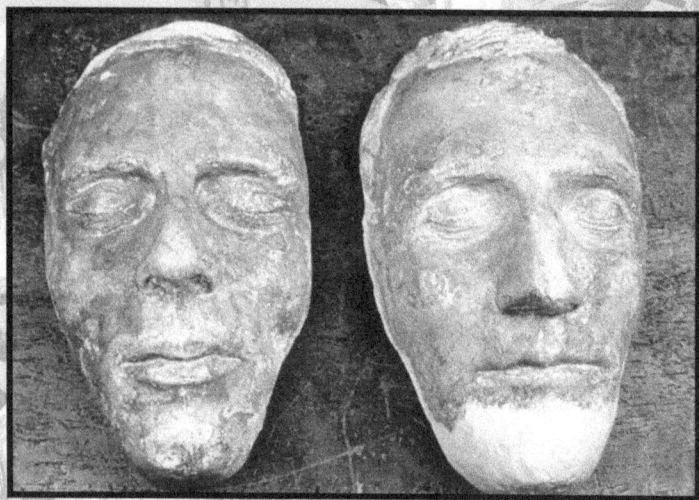

Joseph Smith
1805-1844

Hyrum Smith
1800-1844

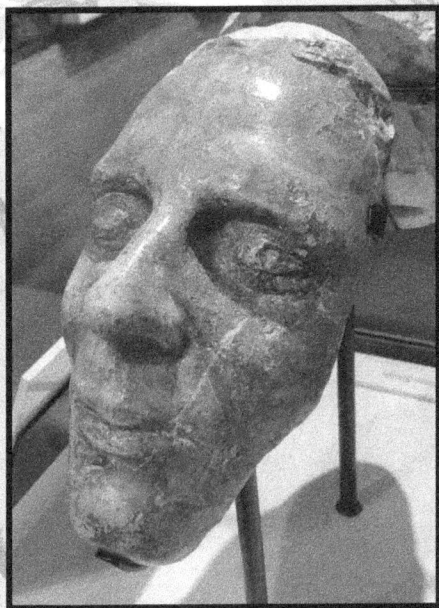

Joseph Smith
1805-1844

Hyrum Smith
1800-1844

John Wesley (87)
June 28, 1703 - March 2, 1791

Claim to fame:
English cleric, theologian, and evangelist who was a leader of a revival movement within the Church of England known as Methodism.

Location of demise:
London, England.

Cause of death:
Unknown, but possibly a stroke.

Final resting place:
Buried at his chapel on City Road, London, England.

Last words:
With his friends gathered around him, Wesley grasped their hands and said repeatedly, "Farewell, farewell." At the end, he said, "The best of all is, God is with us," as he lifted his arms and repeated, "The best of all is, God is with us."

Fun facts:
Wesley coined the phrase "agree to disagree." He had theological differences with a pastor named George Whitefield. When Whitefield died, Wesley gave his memorial sermon, saying: "We may think and let think; we may 'agree to disagree. But, meantime, let us hold fast the essentials."

John Wesley's brother Charles wrote the song Hark, the Herald Angels Sing in 1738.

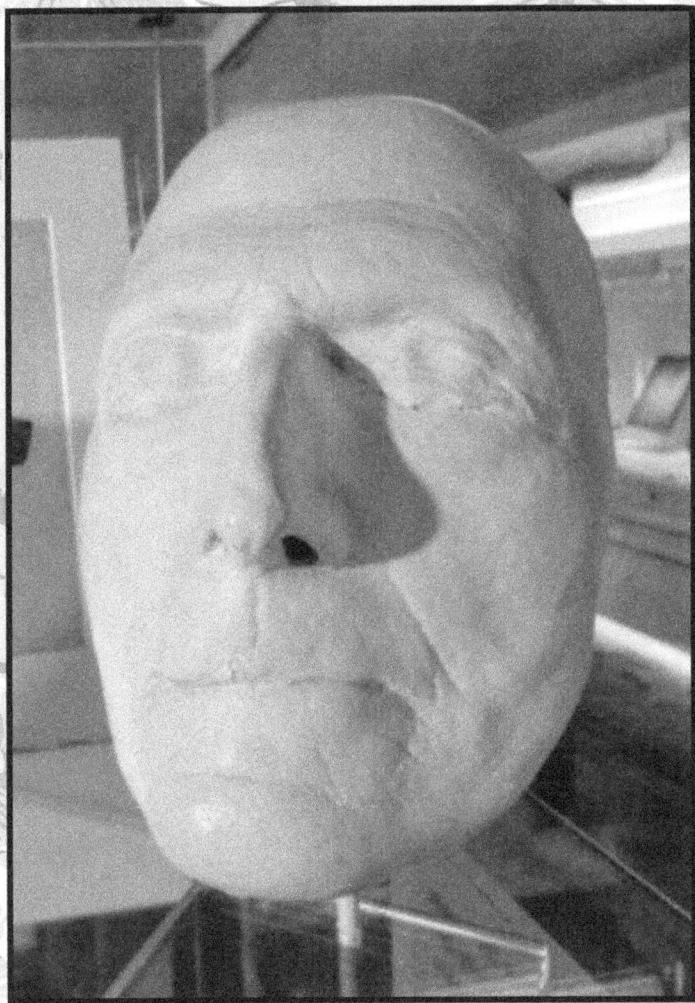

John Wesley
1703-1791

Chapter 9
NO MORE

Including...
Dolly The Sheep
Grace, Lady Manners
Michelangelo Buonarroti
Friedrich Nietzsche
Diego Rivera

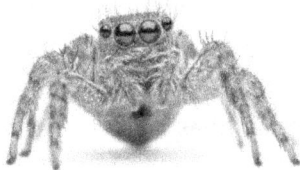

Dolly (6.5)

July 5, 1996 - February 14, 2003

Claim to fame:
A female Finn-Dorset sheep and the first mammal cloned from an adult somatic cell.

Location of demise:
Roslin Institute, Midlothian, Scotland.

Cause of death:
Euthanized. She had a progressive lung disease and severe arthritis. An autopsy revealed she had lung cancer called ovine pulmonary adenocarcinoma, also known as Jaagsiekte, a sheep disease caused by the retrovirus JSRV.

Final resting place:
Taxidermied and put on display at the National Museum of Scotland in Edinburgh, Scotland.

Last words:
"Baa."

Fun facts:
Dolly was named after American singer Dolly Parton, because as her creator Ian Wilmut explained, "Dolly is derived from a mammary gland cell and we couldn't think of a more impressive pair of glands than Dolly Parton's." Dolly Parton's reaction was, "I always said there's no such thing as baaad publicity."

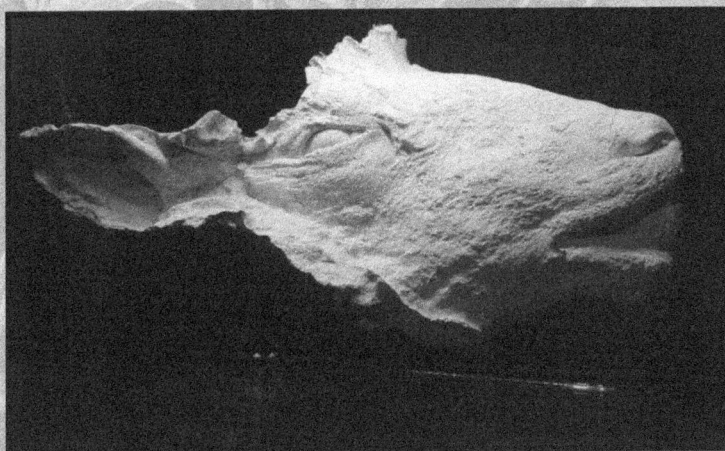

Dolly (Code Name 6LLS)
1996-2003

Grace, Lady Manners (73)
1575 - November 27, 1648

Claim to fame:
English noblewoman who lived at Haddon Hall near Bakewell, Derbyshire. She founded Bakewell's Lady Manners School in 1636.

Location of demise:
Haddon Hall, Bakewell, Derbyshire, England.

Final resting place:
Bakewell Parish Church, Bakewell, Derbyshire, England.

Fun facts:
On August 1, 1593 Grace married a Member of Parliament, Sir George Manners (1569-1623) of Haddon Hall in Derbyshire. The inscription in Bakewell Church says they had nine children; Three sons and six daughters.

In May 1636 Grace, Lady Manners bought some land at Elton which was to provide an annual income of £15 for "the mayntayninge of a Schoolemaister for ever to teach a free Schoole within the Townshippe of Bakewell, for the better instructinge of the male children of the Inhabitants of Bakewell and Great Rowsley aforesaid..."

Grace, Lady Manners
1575-1648

Michelangelo Buonarroti (88)

March 6, 1475 - February 18, 1564

Claim to fame:
Italian sculptor, painter, architect, and poet of the High Renaissance, best known for sculpting The Pieta (1499) and the David (1504), and painting the frescoes of scenes from Genesis on the ceiling of the Sistine Chapel (1512) and The Last Judgment (1541) on its altar wall.

Location of demise:
Rome, Papal States, Lazio, Italy.

Final resting place:
Basilica di Santa Croce, Florence, Tuscany, Italy.

Death mask maker:
Daniele da Volterra.

Last words:
"I'm still learning."

Fun facts:
Pope Pius IV ordered that Michelangelo's body be buried in Rome in St. Peter's Basilica, but Michelangelo's nephew Leonardo Buonarroti fulfilled his uncle's last request, bringing his corpse back to Florence for burial in Santa Croce.

Michelangelo worked until the week he died. His last sculpture was the "Rondanini Pieta," which depicts Jesus in the arms of the Virgin Mary.

Michelangelo Buonarroti
1475-1564

Friedrich Nietzsche (55)

October 15, 1844 - August 25, 1900

Claim to fame:
German philosopher and classical philologist, best known for The Birth of Tragedy (1872), Thus Spoke Zarathustra (1883), Twilight of the Idols (1888), The Antichrist (1888), and Ecce Homo (1908).

Location of demise:
Weimar, Saxe-Weimar-Eisenach, German Empire.

Cause of death:
Pneumonia and multiple strokes.

Final resting place:
Röcken Churchyard, Röcken, Burgenlandkreis, Sachsen-Anhalt, Germany. Nietzsche's sister Elisabeth had him buried beside their father.

Death mask maker:
Curt Stoeving. The original death mask is part of the sculpture collection of the museums of the Klassik Stiftung Weimar.

Last words:
"Mutter, ich bin dumm (Mother, I am dumb)."

Fun facts:
Nietzsche famously declared in his 1882 work, The Gay Science, "God remains dead. And we have killed him." The phrase also appears in Nietzsche's Thus Spoke Zarathustra.

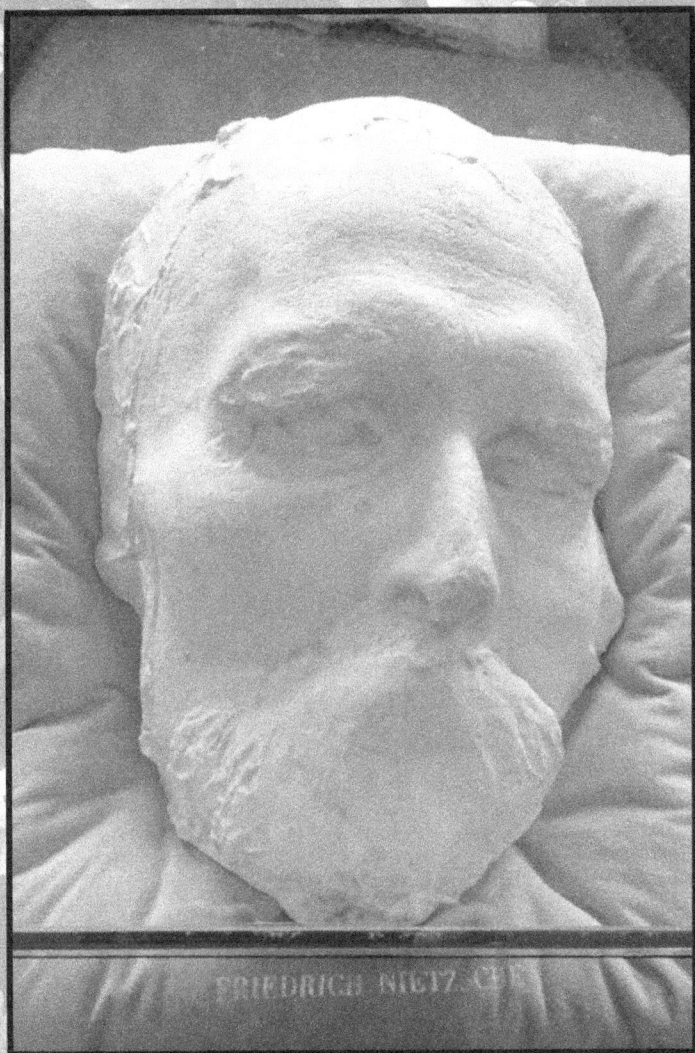

Friedrich Nietzsche
1844-1900

Diego Rivera (70)
December 8, 1886 - November 24, 1957

Claim to fame:
Mexican painter whose frescoes helped establish the mural movement in Mexican and international art, including Detroit Industry Murals (1933) and Man At The Crossroads (1934).

Location of demise:
San Angel, Mexico City, Mexico.

Cause of death:
Heart failure following a period of cancer treatment.

Final resting place:
Panteón de Dolores, Rotonda de las Personas Ilustres (Circle of Illustrious Persons), Miguel Hidalgo borough, Mexico City, Mexico.

Fun facts:
Rivera allegedly ate a handful of his ex-wife Frida Kahlo's cremated remains, fresh from the furnace.

Rivera wanted his ashes to be mixed with those of Frida Kahlo and put in a private temple he had built. The Mexican government instead had him buried in the Rotonda de las Personas Ilustres (Circle of Illustrious Persons).

Rivera had a twin brother called Carlos Maria, who died at the age of one and a half. Rivera's own firstborn son, Diego, died at the age of two.

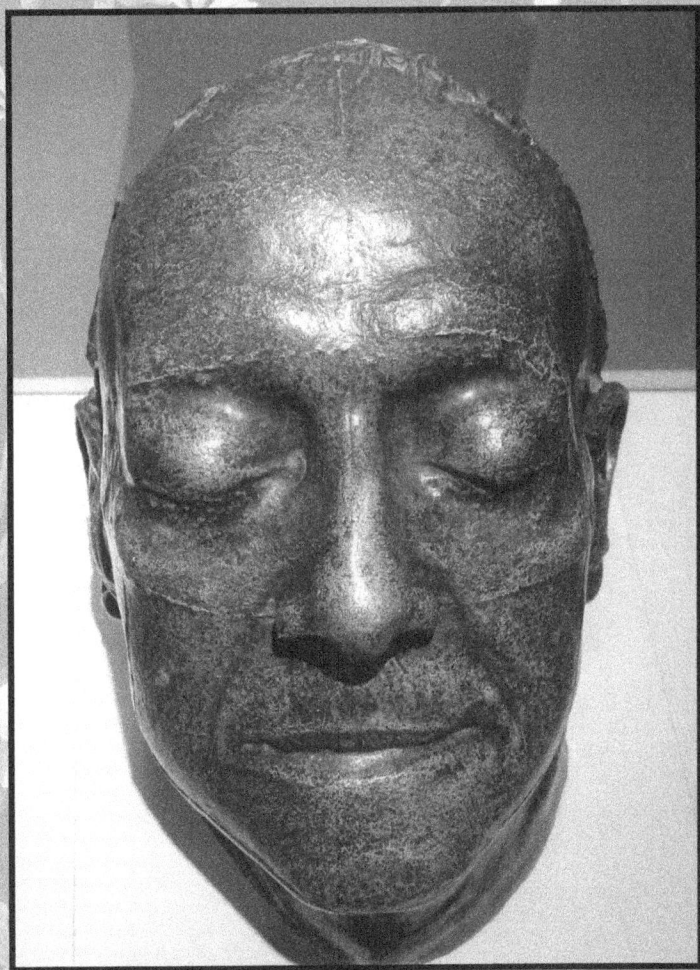

Diego Rivera
1886-1957

157